The Color Nature Library
DOGS

By
PEGGY WRATTEN

Designed by
DAVID GIBBON

Produced by
TED SMART

CRESCENT BOOKS

First published in Great Britain 1977 by Colour Library International Ltd.,
80-82, Coombe Road, New Malden, Surrey, England.

Designed by David Gibbon CLI.   *Produced by* Ted Smart CLI.
© *Text:* Peggy Wratten. © *Illustrations:* Colour Library International.
Printed in Spain by Grijelmo, S. A.
Display and Text filmsetting by Focus Photoset, London, England.

ISBN 0 904681 28 9
COLOUR LIBRARY INTERNATIONAL

The dog was almost certainly the first animal to be fully domesticated. For many thousands of years it has given Man faithful friendship and co-operation. Wild dogs are social animals, living in packs or family groups, showing loyalty to a leader and conforming to the rules of the pack. Even domesticated dogs that have gone feral will readily form packs under a leader, so man found it relatively easy to train dogs to work for him and obey him. Consequently, the traditional role of the dog is a working one.

Over the years different breeds have been selectively developed to serve different purposes. The hound has been used for hunting from prehistoric times down to the present day. The sheepdog was bred especially to herd sheep under the direction of the shepherd. In polar regions, in spite of modern inventions, the husky dog is still used for pulling sledges and, for many years before the advent of the automobile, the dog was used in many countries for draught work. Special breeds with more than average intelligence and learning

left: Old English Sheepdog pup
right: Wire-haired Fox Terrier
below: Shetland Sheepdog and Old English Sheepdog

ability are today trained for police tracking work and crowd control. Guard dogs are valued for guarding large premises at night and even the domestic pet dog will usually alert the household to possible danger by barking. More recently certain breeds have been trained as guide dogs for blind people. No other animal species has rendered such a diversity of service.

It is only in relatively recent times that dogs have been kept solely as domestic pets. Today the dog is a familiar and much loved member of many households all over the world. Many different breeds and varieties have been produced to satisfy man's whims and fancies, as well as his needs, and some pedigree breeds bear little resemblance to their wild ancestors. The Dog Show is now a firmly based institution in many countries.

left: Dalmatian and Smooth-haired Dachshund
right: Welsh Corgi (Cardigan)
below: Welsh Corgi (Pembroke)

Origin and Domestication

The dog first appeared on earth some twenty million years ago and according to the findings of bones in prehistoric middens it probably first became domesticated, at least to some extent, about 10,000 years ago. Some authorities put the time at nearer 15,000 years. The dog was probably first domesticated in the warmer parts of Europe and southwest and southern Asia, judging from firmer evidence based on more complete skeletons dating from about 8000 B.C. This dog was almost certainly of a similar type to the modern pariahs and the Dingo. The latter was almost certainly taken to Australia from Polynesia about 3000 years ago by the ancestors of the present-day Aboriginals. Around this time, too, a second small breed of dog seems to have been bred in Europe. Probably dogs were first kept by man to provide him with food. Even today some primitive people eat dogs. Once man and dog became associated, however, the value of the animal as a hunter, as a guard or as a draught animal probably soon came to be recognized.

Added to the uncertainty as to the period when the dog first became of use to man, there has long been speculation about its origin. There are several theories: that its ancestor was the wolf; that the dog is derived from the wolf with some admixture of jackal; and that the dog came from a wild species distinct from both wolf and jackal, that has since become extinct. From the little real evidence we have, the first of these theories seems the most acceptable especially since the behaviour and characteristics of the wolf have been more extensively studied during recent years. However, it has to be admitted that much of the evidence is purely circumstantial and the correct answer will probably never now be established.

The problem has been made more difficult because no other domestic animal shows so much variation in colour, coat, size and behaviour as the dog. The smallest is the Chihuahua (pronounced chi-wa-wa), a breed developed from the Mexican hairless dog and only 6-9 in high and up to 6 lb weight (sometimes as little as 1½ lb!). The largest are the Mastiff, up to 30 in high and 165 lb weight and the St. Bernard up to 28 in high and 200 lb weight

left above: Pyrenean Mountain Dog
left below: Pointer
right: St. Bernard

The Chief Senses

Smell is a dog's dominant sense, although the degree to which sight is used varies from breed to breed. In general, to a dog the world around presents a pattern of smells just as to us it presents a pattern of visual details. In the best tracker dogs the smelling membrane in the nose contains about 220 million receptor cells compared with only 5 million in the human nose, and each cell works more efficiently than ours.

Like most other mammals, a dog in the wild is a territorial animal and the boundaries of its territory are marked by its urine. The smell of the urine will tell other male dogs to keep away and inform a bitch of the presence of a possible mate. The messages it conveys are, however, much more numerous than this and usually more subtle. Even the domestic dog urinates repeatedly

left: Smooth-haired Dachshunds
right: Scottish Terriers
bottom: Pekingese pups

when taken for a walk to tell other dogs that it has passed that way. When two dogs meet they first sniff noses and then sniff each other's hindquarters for later recognition.

A dog's sense of taste, so closely allied to smell, is not particularly discerning. In fact it has fewer taste buds on the tongue than we have. A dog, like most carnivores, once it has sniffed its food to see that it is to its liking, will swallow it whole with little or no chewing.

Although a dog predominantly uses its sense of smell, its sight is reasonably good and, like cats, it has a faint colour vision. The eyes are positioned to look straight ahead and as would be expected, sight is sharpest in working dogs and sporting dogs. Gun dogs particularly, that point and retrieve game, are almost entirely dependent on vision, at least in the duties for which they are kept.

A dog's sense of hearing is very acute and, like the cat, its hearing extends beyond the range of the human ear into the higher frequencies. The 'silent' dog whistle, inaudible to our ears, is easily heard by canines. Usually dogs with pricked ears have better hearing than those with floppy ears. Hearing is particularly necessary to some working dogs in conjunction with their other senses. Sheepdogs, guard dogs and guide dogs especially need an acute sense of hearing to do their work efficiently.

left: Bearded Collie
bottom: Shetland Sheepdogs
right: Collie pups

Communication

The familiar bark of the domestic dog so expressive of many moods seems only to have developed during domestication because wild dogs do not bark. Small pet dogs seem to bark and yap a lot but the larger working dogs are quieter and bark only when necessary or when excited. The growl is a sign of aggression and the whine a sign of disquiet. Many dogs yawn at each other as wolves do before setting off to hunt.

Apart from vocal sounds, the dog has a whole range of gestures to convey different moods. It will prick its ears at sudden noises, wag its tail when pleased. The way the tail is held is also indicative of mood. It will raise its hackles, stiffen its body, bare its teeth and snarl when about to attack. It will roll over with legs in the air as a sign of submission.

left: Miniature Poodle
right: Standard Poodle
bottom: Toy Poodle pups

top, overleaf: Dobermann Pinscher and Yorkshire Terrier
bottom: Longcoat Chihuahua, Pekingese and St. Bernard
right: Cocker Spaniels

Courtship and Family Life

As a result of domestication the reproductive cycle of the dog has altered from that of its wild counterparts. Sexual maturity occurs earlier in domestic dogs, at one year instead of two. Bitches come into heat twice a year at any season and males are able to mate at any time.

If courtship and mating are allowed naturally, the dog is attracted by the smell of a bitch on heat. He will show increasing interest in her, inviting play by springing up and down on his forelegs in front of her, cocking his head on one side. The male will attempt to mount her but the bitch will not allow mating until she reaches full oestrus. Once receptive the bitch allows the dog to mount her and copulation is unusual in that the pair become locked together (knotted) for about 20 minutes, sometimes for as much as an hour. The gestation of the dog is about 63 days.

A litter may comprise anything up to a dozen or more puppies, the largest recorded being 22. After the birth of each puppy the mother will clean off the birth membranes, bite through the umbilical cord, lick the puppy clean and eat the placenta (afterbirth). The puppy's first reaction is to find a nipple and suck milk from its mother. The puppies are born more or less helpless, blind and deaf. At first the mother stays with them nearly all the time, keeping them warm, suckling and grooming them. When later she leaves them for short periods, they will huddle together for warmth.

The puppies' eyes open at 9 to 14 days and hearing begins at 10 to 12 days. After about three to four weeks the puppies show signs of independence and the mother begins to detach herself from the litter, although she will be quick to help any pup in difficulties. The puppies start trying to feed themselves, although they are not fully weaned until four to eight weeks old. To teach them self-sufficiency the mother cuffs them for any wrongdoing, she teaches them to keep the sleeping basket clean and joins in their play. Much as the puppies seem to enjoy their play, in the wild this would be a preparation for adult life and even in domestic dogs the play shows all the pattern of the dog's hunting behaviour.

After about eight weeks the puppies will be fully independent of their mother.

left: Bulldog
top right: Boston Terrier
middle right: Pug
bottom right: Bulldog

Hunting and Feeding

Although today the family dog is fed mainly from tins of prepared food and its meals are regular and sufficient, almost any dog, given the opportunity, will go out hunting into the fields and woods.

Being a carnivore, the dog gulps its food with little or no chewing, but it loves to gnaw a bone and will bury it in the garden for future enjoyment. A dog's teeth are characteristic of a carnivore: incisors for gripping small prey, dagger-like canines for making slashing cuts at large prey or enemies and cheekteeth which include the carnassials for slicing flesh or crunching bones.

It is said that half the small dogs at a vet's surgery today are there because of gum disease caused by too easy a diet. If dogs do not use their teeth properly to tear flesh and crack bones or hard biscuits, the teeth become encrusted with tartar. This inflames the gums and teeth may have to be extracted. However, dogs need never wear dentures, they can manage perfectly well without teeth!

left: King Charles Spaniels
bottom, left: Pomeranian
bottom, right: Cocker Spaniel
right: Cocker Spaniel

Intelligence

The dog has always been thought to be highly intelligent, at least by its owner, largely because it is usually trainable, obedient and able to learn simple tricks. This does not by any means prove that a dog is intelligent, however, and some scientists have even gone so far as to deny that any animal, other than a human, can show intelligence.

One of the many definitions of intelligence is that it is the ability to recognise a problem, formulate a solution and quickly act upon it. The working sheepdog seems to prove by its cleverness and initiative that it is indeed capable of this. There are many stories of a sheepdog being ordered to go out on a pitch-black night to round up a flock that had scattered widely. By daylight, unassisted, the sheepdog had rounded them all up. Anyone who has watched sheepdog trials can testify to the sheepdog's ability to use its initiative to solve a difficult problem of herding.

There are many other stories of other breeds of dog alerting their owners to danger of fire or disaster and helping humans selflessly without any regard for their own safety.

Four pictures of Alsatians

Types of breeds

The classification of breeds of dogs has always presented problems ever since different breeds were recognized. Today this classification varies in different countries. There are over a hundred distinct breeds now recognized, more if one includes varieties of breeds, and a convenient grouping, which does not of course satisfy everyone, is recognized by the American Kennel Club. It indicates broadly the uses to which the various dogs are put as follows:

1. Sporting breeds: includes Pointers, Retrievers, Setters and Spaniels.
2. Hound breeds: includes those hounds that use scent such as Bloodhound, Foxhound and Beagle, and those that use sight such as Greyhound, Afghan, Borzoi and Dachshund.
3. Working breeds: includes those used as sledge dogs, sheepdogs, guide dogs, St. Bernard and Boxer.

left: Irish or Red Setter
right: English Setters
bottom: Gordon Setter

4. Terrier breeds: familiar small dogs such as Fox Terrier and Scottish Terrier.
5. Toy Dogs: includes the Pekingese and Chihuahua.
6. Non-sporting Dogs: includes those difficult to classify elsewhere such as the Bulldog, Dalmation and Poodle.

left: Border Collie
below: Collies herding sheep
right: Rough Collie

Sporting Dogs

To assist him when out shooting game-birds, man has trained sporting dogs to find and flush the birds and, although they do not assist in the actual killing, they help to find dead or wounded game. In Britain they are known as Gundogs.

At the start of the shoot, the Pointer or Setter ranges widely to get an airborne scent of the bird long before it is alarmed enough to fly to safety. They then come to a complete stop and remain rigid, pointing in the direction of the game until the 'gun' comes up, when they either lead him nearer the game until the bird flies, or drop to the ground at the shot.

The Pointer is thought to have originally come from Spain and been evolved especially for work with game-birds, able to gallop fast and range widely over fields and moors and with excellent sight and smell. Well-built, with high head-carriage and a long, muscular neck, it is a big dog standing 24 to 27in. at the shoulder, with a short fine coat.

The English, Irish and Gordon Setters are similar in build to the Pointer but the head is longer and finer-skulled and the coat long. The Gordon Setter, bred for the Scottish moors is particularly strongly built with a heavy coat.

The Retriever walks at heel or sits by its master until the bird is shot when it is ordered to pick up the game, either dead or wounded, and bring it back. The Retrievers are all large, active dogs, with good heads and necks, strong bodies and muscular hindquarters. The muzzles are wide, suitable for carrying any size of bird. The Golden Retriever, so popular as a domestic pet, is also a good gundog with a soft mouth. The Labrador Retrievers either Black or Golden are both great gundogs with wonderful noses for finding game. They have a dense undercoat to keep them warm when swimming even in icy waters.

The Spaniel does not lead its handler to the game like the Pointer but hunts about close to the 'gun' until it has found and flushed a bird, then after the game is shot, retrieves it to hand. The Cocker Spaniel with a height of 15-16in., is a lively, active dog, very strong and muscular for its size. Originally bred in Britain for flushing woodcock, it is now bred mainly for show and as a companion.

left: Boxer pups
right, top: Bloodhounds
right, below: Boxer

Hounds

Probably man's first use of the dog, apart from using it as food, was for hunting. As the dog is by nature a hunter it would have required little training for this. It is thought that the first breed used was possibly of the greyhound type. Today, different varieties of hound are still used by man for the chase, although most of them will also settle down quite happily to a domestic life, if given plenty of exercise. There are two types of hound: those that hunt by scent and those that hunt by sight.

Most of the scent hounds are of ancient origin. The Basset Hound as long ago as the 16th century was used in France to hunt badgers, wolves and smaller animals. It is a handsome hound, with long droopy ears and a soulful expression. The long body, only 12-18in. at the shoulder, the short sturdy hindlegs and crooked forelegs make it seem slightly out of proportion. It is still used as a pack hound for hunting on foot but also makes a splendid family pet. The Beagle is another ancient

left: Golden Retriever
right: Deerhound
bottom: Great Dane

breed used today, particularly in Britain, for hunting on foot like the Basset Hound. Beagles are compactly built, active hounds with a wide domed head and long ears. They are particularly attractive as puppies. The Bloodhound is the oldest of the scent hounds. With a heavy build and large head it has folds of loose skin falling over the forehead and sides of the face. It has been used particularly for tracking down criminals.

Although viewed with disfavour by the conservationists, hunting the fox, deer and otter with the help of pack hounds still goes on in Britain and in other countries, although not so frequently as in former years. The modern Foxhound in England has the reputation of being the most efficient working animal used by man. The American Foxhound is similar but a heavier animal. All Foxhounds need good noses, good staying power and good voices to co-operate with the huntsmen. Although the Dachshund was first bred in Germany as a badger dog to go down holes it is today popular as a companion and show dog. It is characterised by its long body and very short legs and is familiarly called a 'sausage dog'.

All the sight hounds are bred for speed. One of the most popular today as a show dog and one of the most beautiful is the Afghan Hound. In its native Afghanistan it is used as a guard dog and for hunting deer and wolves. Shaped rather like a Greyhound it stands 24-29in. high and has a long, thick, silky coat. The Borzoi, or Russian Wolfhound, is perhaps the most elegant of all hounds and one of the swiftest. Originally kept in packs by the Russian nobles for hunting wolves, it is now a popular show dog in Britain and the United States. Similar in build but smaller the Saluki has also become popular in recent years. It is the modern coursing dog of the Arabs.

Of all the swift hounds perhaps the Greyhound has altered least over the years. It was once used for coursing the hare and, in Ancient Egypt, for running down the gazelle. Today it is popular as a racing animal on the Greyhound track in the United States and Britain, where Greyhound racing has become big business. Greyhounds are easily recognized by their long sharp muzzles, long bodies, arched loins, very long limbs and long thin tails.

left, top: Pointer
left, below: Smooth-haired Fox Terrier
right: Basset Hound

Working Dogs

The name for this group of dogs is not very satisfactfory as originally all breeds of dog worked for man. However, it is convenient to include in this group such working dogs as sheepdogs, guard dogs, draught dogs and guide dogs.

left: Beagle pups
bottom: Bearded Collie pups
right: English Cocker Spaniel

Sheepdogs and Herders

It must have been many thousands of years ago when man first trained dogs to herd and guard his flocks. This was a remarkable achievement, going against a dog's natural instincts, as cattle and sheep would have been its natural prey. Today there are sheepdogs or herding dogs all over the world and their ability and intelligence while at work are supreme among dogs. Any sheepdog trial will demonstrate this. The Collie breeds are universally known and although they make good family dogs and show dogs they are at their best as working sheepdogs. The Rough Collie is still used in Austrailia for controlling large flocks of sheep. In Britain most of

left: Dalmatian
right: English Springer Spaniel
bottom: Rough Collie, Great Dane, Border Terrier, Boston Terrier, Smooth-haired Fox Terrier, Borzoi, Alsatian.
overleaf top, left: Dalmatian pup
top, right: Jack Russell Terrier pups
right: Great Dane and pups
bottom: Golden Cocker Spaniel pups

the working sheepdogs are Welsh or Border Collies. Renowned for intelligence, stamina and speed, they excel at obedience trials. The Shetland Sheepdog or 'Sheltie' was originally used in the Shetland Isles for herding sheep but today, like the Old English Sheepdog it is more popular as a family pet dog. The beautiful Pyrenean Mountain Dog with thick long white coat and dense neck frill was used in the Middle Ages to protect flocks from bears and wolves, as a dog of war armed with a spiked collar, and for guard work. It still serves as a guide and pack dog today.

Some dogs were bred as cattle herders. Most famous, but rarely used for this purpose today, are the Welsh Cardigan and Pembroke Corgis. They were used in cattle droves from Wales to Smithfield Market in London and were known as heelers as they nipped the heels of stragglers. With bat ears, compact bodies and short coats, the Corgis stand only 12in. at the shoulder and make excellent house dogs for small homes. The only active cattle-herding breed in the world today is the Australian Cattle Dog. A large dog standing 18in. at the shoulder and weighing 40lb. this sturdy dog has been bred to cope with the strain and heat of cattle-driving.

left: English Setter
right: Black Labrador Retriever
bottom: Yellow Labrador Retriever

Guard Dogs, Police Dogs and Guide Dogs

When man first trained dogs to guard his home and property he did not find it a difficult task as a dog naturally has a well-developed sense of territory. In Ancient Egypt and Rome guard dogs were used extensively. They were large, powerful animals of the Mastiff type. Today, first among the guard dogs is the Alsatian or German Shepherd Dog. First used as a herd dog, the Alsatian is intelligent, reliable and strong. It is used by the Police and the Military and is also used as a guide dog for the blind. It is invaluable to the Police for tracking and crowd control. Although also popular as a family pet, many people distrust it, probably because of its wolf-like looks. Other German breeds seem to excel at guarding and Police work. The Dobermann Pinscher makes a splendid guard dog and is used in Police work in Europe and the United States. The Great

left: Borzoi
bottom right: Salukis
bottom left: Afghan Hound
right: Greyhound

Dane was once used for fighting and hunting and is still used sometimes today for guarding because of its formidable size, yet it is not in any way a ferocious animal and makes a good family dog if it has plenty of room for exercise. The Boxer, with its broad square head and muzzle, smooth short coat and well-muscled body has a reputation for affection and reliability and some have been trained as guide dogs for the blind.

In time of war dogs have been used for rescue work, particularly as a help to Red Cross workers, finding wounded and leading ambulance workers to them.

Another dog with a reputation as a guide dog is the St. Bernard. Although it was supposed to be sent out from the St. Bernard Monastery, in the Swiss Alps, to find lost travellers in the snow, this story is now discounted because the St. Bernard is of such a massive build that it would have quickly sunk in the snow and its thick coat would have become clogged. It was however, used to guide monks up and down the mountain passes.

left: Weimaraner
right: Pyrenean Mountain Dog
bottom: Dobermann Pinscher

Draught Dogs

The use of dogs for haulage seems to have been confined mainly to Europe and the polar regions. In Europe today the dog is still seen occasionally pulling milk-carts and bakers' vans but the practice is dying out. The Leonberger, rather like a large Golden Retriever, has been used for this work in parts of northern Europe and the Bernese Mountain Dog was a popular Swiss draught dog.

Today the only dogs still used extensively for pulling loads are the 'Huskies' of the Arctic and Antarctic regions. They are invaluable for pulling sleds and will work till they drop in fifty-below-zero temperatures. Although popularly all sled dogs are called 'Huskies' there are many distinct breeds in regular use as sled dogs. The best sled dogs are fairly short and sturdy with thick coats to keep out the cold. They must have powerful chest muscles for pulling and plenty of stamina to keep going for many miles on a very limited fish diet.

left: Shih Tzu pup
bottom: Yorkshire Terrier
right: Border Terrier

above: Chow
left: Boxer

above: Airedale Terrier
bottom: Bulldog, Rough Collie

Terriers

Terriers, generally, are among the hardiest of all dogs. They were originally bred for entering fox earths and badger setts and for the destruction of vermin. They are all fairly small dogs, sturdy and robust with a strong body and rather long head, some long-legged, some short-legged. Most varieties have short, rough coats. Above all they are active, enthusiastic dogs with an eagerness for work and a very friendly nature. Although most of them today, whether pedigree or merely 'mongrel', are household pets, they are at their best when working. Even the domesticated Terrier, on seeing a rat or mouse, will instinctively chase and kill it.

The Terrier was originally a British breed and at one time nearly every district in the country had its own individual variety. Today, many breeds are popular on the Continent, in the United States and other countries. There is only room here to describe a few.

Scotland is the home of many rough-haired, short-legged Terriers. Probably the original was the Cairn Terrier. It is a good sturdy game-working dog and

left: Rough Collie
bottom: Husky Dogs
right: Cairn Terrier and
West Highland White Terrier

excellent ratter. Its coat is harsh and thick with a dense undercoat. Although very popular as a pet it is at its best when working. The Scottish Terrier or 'Scottie' is one of the most popular Terriers. It is small with a very long head and short legs and a thick wiry coat, usually black. It is popular as a show dog or companion in Britain and the United States.

One of the longer-legged Terriers is the Airedale Terrier from Yorkshire. It is the largest of the British Terriers and was widely used as an army dog in World War I. The head is long with a long powerful muzzle. The coat is short and rough. The Airedale Terrier is not so popular as formerly as a family dog but is still used occasionally as a guard dog.

The Smooth-haired Fox Terrier is one of the best-known of all the Terriers and popular today in many countries. Although an excellent companion in a town house, it is a very capable ratter in the country. The head is flat and narrow with strong jaws and small ears that drop forwards. The very short smooth coat is white, marked with black or tan.

left: Pointer
right: Harlequin Great Dane
bottom: St. Bernard

Toy Dogs

The Toy Dogs today are bred solely as pets. They have no other purpose in life except to give pleasure, especially to ladies. Some breeds are so small as to seem almost grotesque.

Of all the Toy breeds one of the most popular and one of the smallest is the Yorkshire Terrier. Although originally used by Yorkshire mill workers for catching mice and rats in the woollen factories, today Yorkshire Terriers are kept solely as pets or show dogs. The coat is normally long, straight and glossy, a dark steel blue with tan on the chest. Some specimens are bred as small as 2-4lb.

The Pekingese, a firm favourite, and pampered pet of women in many countries is, in fact, one of the oldest breeds of small dog. It has a Chinese ancestry dating back to the 8th century. Small varieties were called 'Sleeve Pekes' and were carried in the wide sleeves of the Mandarins. It is a member of the Spaniel family and has a long straight coat with a profuse mane forming a frill round the neck. The head is wide with a short muzzle and large eyes.

left: Beagle
bottom: a gathering of Foxhounds
right: a working English Springer Spaniel

The origin of the Pug is rather obscure but it is said to have been brought from China by Dutch traders. It has an affectionate and gentle nature but is more popular on the Continent than in Britain or the United States. It has all the features of a miniature Mastiff with a round head, short muzzle and wrinkled face, short square body and strong legs.

The smallest dog in the world is the Chihuahua originating from Mexico and now very popular in the United States. One specimen has been recorded as weighing only 24 oz, an appalling example of the dictates of fashion. Most are, however, between 2 and 6 lb. There are two varieties: Long-coated and Short-coated. The head is round with large erect ears and prominent eyes. The coat is usually white with tan, blue or black markings. Although comfort-loving, male Chihuahuas may be aggressive and fight other males or females.

left: Long-haired Dachshund puppy
bottom: Poodle
right: Yellow Labrador Retrievers

Non-sporting Dogs

This group, sometimes called Utility Dogs, contains those breeds excluding the Toys, that are simply household pets and companions and are not used by man for sport or for herding or any other utilitarian purpose. They are no less popular or attractive.

Perhaps the best-known and most popular are the Poodles. They are very suitable for town houses and flats because of their small size and because they do not smell or moult, although they should have daily brushing to keep their coats in good condition. They are bred in Standard (large) and Miniature (medium) and there is also a very small one that is classified under Toy Dogs.

left: Irish or Red Setter
right: Smooth-haired Dachshund
(black and tan)
bottom: Bloodhound

The Poodle was originally a Water Spaniel from Germany and clipped to facilitate swimming. If not clipped into too grotesque a fashion the Poodle is a very attractive dog.

A dog very popular in the United States is the Boston Terrier. It looks more like a Bulldog and was originally produced by crossing English and French Bulldogs and Old English Terriers. Also included in this group is the Bulldog, one of Britain's oldest breeds and accepted as the British 'National dog'.

left: West Highland White Terrier puppy
right: West Highland White Terrier
bottom: Cairn Terrier
overleaf:
top left: Shetland Sheepdog
top right: Airedale Terrier
bottom: Yellow Labrador Retriever
right: Shetland Sheepdogs

The Family Dog

Much has been said in this book about different breeds of dogs and especially those that man uses to work for him. Perhaps now we should end with a few words about the ordinary family dog, be it pedigree or just plain 'mongrel'. The relationship between man and his dog companion is unique. If given a good home, regular food and exercise and, especially, friendly treatment the dog will repay you with years of faithful service. It will sit with its head on your feet when you are relaxing in the evening by the fire or will run joyously before you when taken for a walk in the countryside. It may even catch the odd mouse or rat and bark to warn you of visitors or strangers to the house.

The dog, unlike the cat, however, is far happier if its owner trains it to be obedient and if done wisely and well the dog will not only love its master but will also respect him.

below: Clumber Spaniel pups
right: Bloodhound

INDEX

Photographs supplied by:
Colour Library International Ltd., 80-82 Coombe Road, New Malden, Surrey, England.
and
Bruce Coleman Ltd., 16a-17a Windsor Street, Uxbridge, Middlesex, England.